Moose Mania

Cover Illustration by Margarita Sikorskaia

Softcover ISBN 13: 978-0-9857179-9-5
Hardcover ISBN 13: 978-1-7327646-9-9

Printed in the United States of America

Cover and interior design by James Monroe Design, LLC.

Lucky Luke, LLC.
4335 Matthew Court
Eagan, Minnesota 55123

www.KevinLovegreen.com
Quantity discounts available!

Chapter 1

The bonfire crackled and sparks raced into the black night sky on this late September night. Crystal, Mel, Reed and I were all staring into the dancing flames, while listening intently to Dad's story. He was describing how the huge black bear took over an hour to finally walk within bow range of his stand. We are at my favorite place on earth, our hunting property in Minnesota. Mel, my dad's good friend was sitting across the fire from me, still dressed in full camo. His son Reed, who is the spitting image of his dad and one of my best hunting buddies, was sitting to my right. With his long lanky legs, it was hard for him to keep his boots out of the fire. Mel kept reminding him to be careful, so he didn't melt the rubber soles of his favorite boots. My sister Crystal was sitting next to Dad, with her camo hat covering up some of her long red hair. There aren't many girls who have as much fun hunting, four wheeling and ramming around in the outdoors as Crystal. This was her second year trying to bag a black bear. She told Dad the boys at school didn't believe she would have the guts to shoot a bear, and Crystal was determined to prove them wrong.

After the second or third version of the bear hunt tale was told, Dad changed the tune and asked Mel when he thought the time would be right to take the kids on a big adventure. Reed and I perked up and were listening closely to see where this conversation led.

"What do you have in mind?" Mel asked.

"I don't know, what about doing something crazy like taking the kids to Colorado or Alberta?" Dad said.

"Where can we go to get a big bear?" Crystal wanted to know.

The dads both looked at each other. "Alaska," they said in unison.

"Alaska!" I shouted.

"That would be so sick!" Reed said with a surprising amount of energy for how late it was getting. "I have seen some of the most amazing hunting shows about Alaska. You are in the middle of nowhere and anything can happen. You can see grizzly bear, black bear, timberwolves and the biggest moose ever," Reed went on.

"Moose?" Crystal's eyes lit up. "Let's go hunting for a moose, Dad!"

"Okay, okay, hold your horses, this was just a fun discussion. Let's get to bed. Mel and I will talk about this more tomorrow and see if it makes any sense."

Reed and I headed for the hose to fill the bucket and put out the fire. We couldn't stop talking about the endless possibilities that might happen on such an adventure. We both knew we needed to keep the pressure on first thing in the morning, this trip had to happen.

Chapter 2

It was hard to believe a whole year had passed and now our same group—Mel, Reed, Dad, Crystal, and I—were standing on a small dirt runway in the middle of Alaska. We'd left Minnesota over fourteen hours ago. Our first landing was in Anchorage, the largest city in Alaska. We then hopped on a plane and touched down in this tiny village called Aniak. Now we are waiting for our third pilot to unload our gear. Each plane has gotten smaller, the farther we have journeyed into nowhere. Other than mosquitoes and pine trees, there was nothing else around us in this little field at the end of the runway.

It was the perfect fall temperature and the afternoon sun was shining bright. I couldn't help but think this was a magical day, and one of many to come. The pilot hopped in the side door and started shoving out our gear like he was a machine. Quickly learning the game, we all lined up ready for the next bag. The plane was just about empty when a red four wheeler came motoring through the trees with a black trailer bouncing behind it. The driver pulled up next to our pile of stuff and turned off the engine. He was a skinny guy with a scruffy short beard, a well-faded camo ball cap, a red and white checkered flannel shirt, and blue jeans that looked like they hadn't been washed for a long time. If I had to guess, he might be around my dad's age, but definitely looked like he had been out here a while.

"Hey Todd, looks like you brought me another batch of fine-looking hunters," he said.

The pilot was kneeling in the doorway of the plane, a bead of sweat running down his forehead.

"You got that right Mitch. I think they're ready for some time in the bush."

"No one threw up on the flight, did they?" Mitch looked right at Reed.

"Not a chance," Reed said, trying to be tough.

"That's good. That was your first little test to see if you're ready for a week in the bush with bear, rain and wolves. I figure if I get someone with a weak stomach I better keep a closer eye on them," he said. "I'm Mitch, and I'm glad you're here"

7

He was off the four wheeler now, shaking our hands. When he got to Crystal he stopped.

"Now this is what we need more of. Women brave enough to get out here and enjoy this great country. What's your name young lady?"

"I'm Crystal."

"It's a pleasure to meet you Crystal," he said. "And I'm guessing you're probably the best shot out of these characters."

"I do all right. I have done a lot of practicing and my dad has taught me well."

"I bet he has. At any rate, welcome, I'm glad to have ya."

"Thanks. I'm really excited to be here."

"Stack your gear in the trailer and let's get out of Todd's way so he can get back at it," Mitch said after meeting everyone.

In a flash, all the gear was stacked high in the trailer. Mitch started the four wheeler and slowly crawled down the trail heading through the trees. After a quick wave to the pilot, we fell in line like circus elephants behind Mitch. I was anxious to see what kind of structures were built so far from civilization.

Chapter 3

We came around a bend in the trail and there was a log cabin that looked like it could be in the pages of a history book. The wood was weathered grey, and whoever built it did not want to waste trees. Sitting out in a small field next to the cabin was a white two-seater plane that looked like it could be in an air show. There was a shed tucked over to the side, near the trees, and the logs were doing all they could to keep it standing. As we arrived, an older guy with grey rugged hair, a thick beard, and wearing mountain clothes stepped out of the cabin.

"Welcome," the man said leisurely, as if he were in no hurry at all.

We each sent him a greeting back.

"Crystal, you, Luke and your dad, come into the cabin and we'll get your licenses taken care of. Mel and Reed, we'll get to you next. Jack here will give you guys a hand sorting bags."

"Okay," Mel said.

I followed Mitch, Dad, and Crystal through the front door where Dad had to duck down a little so he didn't hit his head. Stepping inside, felt like stepping back in time. The smell of a wood burning fireplace fit the place just right. There was only one little table with three chairs, in what I guess was the kitchen. The cabin's only window allowed just enough light for us to see and there were two little bedrooms without doors. Each one had one small bed and a nightstand. One bed was made up and the other had the covers pulled over, like someone had just gotten out of it. Furs and a couple of steel traps hanging from the walls were the only decorations, but they seemed to be all the decorating this place needed.

"Have a seat," Mitch nodded to Dad.

Dad sat down while Crystal and I stood behind him. Mitch went over to a small desk and pulled out a handful of white paper. It would have been more fitting if the papers were faded brown and water stained. Mitch brought the papers to the table, sat down, and started to sort through them.

"Remind me again who's hunting what," Mitch said.

"We are all getting moose tags," Dad clarified. "Crystal and Luke are also getting black bear tags."

Because I was excited, I thought it took way too long to get the licenses filled out. The good news was we were now legal to hunt in Alaska.

We creaked open the door and headed outside, where the sun collided with our eyes.

"You're up," Dad said to Mel and Reed.

"What's with the five piles?" Crystal asked, seeing our gear all divided up.

"One at a time, Mitch will fly us to our camps, each with a small load of gear. Jack had us divide everything up so we were ready to go," Reed explained.

"Jack, can you get Mel and his son's licenses filled out so I can load the plane and get going?" Mitch asked.

"Sure can," Jack said.

Mitch took charge and loaded the plane as if he knew where each piece was intended to go. Minutes later, he had Dad tucked in the rear seat.

"I'll be back in about half an hour. Stand clear, I'm going to start her up," Mitch said as he hopped up into the front seat.

Crystal and I scooted back toward the cabin. The engine sputtered twice and then shot to life. The little prop on the front sped around until you couldn't see it anymore. Dad gave us thumbs up through the window. We both excitedly shot our thumbs up. The plane turned and bounced across the field around the corner and onto the landing strip. Crystal and I raced down the trail, keeping an eye on the plane.

Mitch never paused; he revved up the engine and like someone lifted the plane into the sky, it was airborne and gaining altitude. I have never seen a plane get off the ground in such a short distance.

"That was crazy. How did it get in the air so quick?" Crystal asked.

"I have no idea, but it was awesome," I said.

Chapter 4

The next couple of hours drove Reed and me crazy. We were the last two to go out and I let him go first. His dad was waiting for him at their camp, and he had been there quite a while.

When Mitch returned half an hour later, I finally felt like I was a part of the adventure again. I anxiously hopped up into the plane. I thought I knew what to expect because I had seen the plane come and go four times already. But when it lifted off the ground it was a whole new experience. It was like we were floating across the air and barely moving. My eyes were filled with excitement as I watched every opening below us, knowing I was going to see all kinds of animals from up here. The vast number of trees, hills, rivers and small lakes was overwhelming. I felt so small sitting in this tiny plane looking down at the endless landscape.

"Down there!" Mitch said loudly so I could hear him over the engine.

"Cool!" I shot back as I looked down at a black bear mom and two small cubs in a river.

I strained my neck keeping an eye on the bear as the plane continued on its mission to get me to camp, where Dad and Crystal were waiting.

A few minutes later I heard Mitch shout, "That's what you're looking for!"

He turned the plane so the right side was tilted down. There were two big white blobs that looked very different than the plush green that was painted everywhere else.

"What are those white things?" I asked.

"That's a giant bull moose," Mitch answered.

My eyes strained to focus and now I could make out the distinct outline of two antlers that looked like paddles and a black body. The moose didn't look real to me from up in the sky, and it seemed too small. I had to believe Mitch, though, because he's the expert and has been doing this for a long time.

"Why does it look small?" I had to question.

"Trust me, that bull is huge. You just wait until you get close to him. You'll see what I'm talking about."

Mitch leveled the plane out and then started dropping altitude. I then saw a green tent and realized that Crystal and

Dad were standing next to it. We did a half circle around camp and then dropped from the sky as if we were a goose landing in a small pond. The plane touched the ground, bounced once, and then Mitch slammed the brakes on and we came to a skidding halt.

"Whoa! That was crazy!" I said, shaking my head and swallowing hard.

"Always exciting around here. Wait until we get some wind, then you'll be in for a ride!" Mitch said.

As soon as the engine was cut, Mitch jumped out of the front seat. He opened my door and I crawled out from the tight quarters.

"Hey buddy, how was the ride?" Crystal asked.

"Super cool. Did you guys see the moose?"

"Sure did. Did you happen to see my name on his side?" Crystal asked.

"What? Your name?" I was confused.

"That baby is mine!" Crystal said with a wicked smile on her face.

"Riiiiiiiiiiiight. We'll see," I said.

"Looks like you have your hands full there, Luke," Mitch said tilting his head down with focused eyes.

"Yeah, yeah," I said as I grabbed a bag from Mitch.

We had the plane unloaded and our gear spread out around the tent. Mitch flipped over two white five-gallon buckets and sat down on one of them.

"Pull up a seat," he said to Dad.

Dad plopped down and Mitch started to explain what we had in camp as far as food and supplies. He then gave us the lay of the land by pointing out different landmarks around us.

"The most important thing is to stay together, mark camp on your GPS, and don't go more than a mile away from camp,' Mitch said.

"Why is that?" Dad asked, confused.

"If you shoot a moose, the three of you have to get the meat back to camp so I can pick it up. And trust me, you don't want to haul a moose more than a mile. Now, if you shoot a black bear, you can either skin it where you shot it or drag it back to camp and I will skin it for you."

"This has been one of my best spots over the years. It's a natural funnel through the valley and the moose like to travel through here. If you're patient, eventually one should wonder by. You will find the black bear scattered throughout the hillside eating blueberries. If you spot a good one, have at it."

"Are there any tricks to knowing if it's a good one?" I asked.

"It's very simple. If its head looks small, it's a big one," Mitch said.

I wasn't going to forget that tip. My goal was to track down a big Alaskan bear and take it with my bow. Now I knew what to look for.

Mitch suddenly stood up and popped the top off his bucket. Then he reached in and pulled out two long yellow nylon ribbons. "These are my signals. If you need me for any reason, tie them to that wind sock over there. My plan, depending on weather—and everything depends on weather around here—is to fly over about every two days."

There was an orange cone-looking thing attached to a stick out in the middle of the field. "What's that for?" Crystal asked.

"That little baby lets me know what direction the wind is coming from. My plane does real good landing into the wind, not so good in a side wind."

"Got it," she said.

"I am assuming we want to move in that bull's direction tomorrow and do some calling?" Dad said.

"That's what I would do. They are in the middle of the rut and sounding like a cow moose is your best bet. That's the girl moose," he said, looking at me.

"You will know when a bull has decided to come in. These big boys are not so delicate. That's about it. Have fun, be safe, and remember that bears don't like to be surprised, so be careful going through the thick stuff. I usually do a lot of talking to them when I'm in the bush."

"What do you mean by that?" I asked.

"If it's thick and they can't see me coming, I call out, 'Hey bear, here I come bear,' and that usually does it," he explained.

Crystal and I looked at each other a little puzzled and wondered if he was pulling our legs. But he didn't seem like the kidding type, and there wasn't any chuckle after he said it.

Mitch shook hands with each of us and was back in his plane, not wanting to waste any more time. The plane sputtered to life, bounced down to the end of the field, turned around, and revved up. Then, like it was kind of in slow motion, Mitch drove across the field and lifted into the sky in a super short distance. I could not believe the plane could take off going so slow. It seemed to crawl into the air as it gained altitude. We all three watched closely as he became smaller and smaller in the sky.

"Well, I sure hope we see him again," Dad said.

"I was thinking the same thing, but didn't want to say it," Crystal said, looking a little concerned.

"You guys worry too much, we will be fine. He has done this hundreds of times. Right Dad?" I looked at Dad for a little reinforcement.

"Absolutely!" Dad said like a used car salesman.

Chapter 5

Following a group high-five and a pep talk from Dad, it was time to organize camp. After analyzing how little space we had in the tent, we decided our sleeping bags should be stacked up on one side, leaving enough space to cook and move around. Dad sorted through the food to get an idea of what we had. Anxious to make sure my bow was still sighted in, I went out and found an old stump to shoot at. I opened my bow case and pulled out my release, bow, range finder, and an arrow. I walked back about thirty steps from the stump and used my range finder to laser the distance. The view finder showed me thirty three yards. I nocked the arrow, pulled it back, and held steady. I triggered the release, shooting the arrow. It hit with a thud right in the middle of the stump. Feeling good about the shot, I hurried forward to grab my arrow, which was buried deep in the dry soft wood. I set my bow down and pulled the arrow with both hands. At first it didn't seem to want to budge. I bore down and gave it all I had. Suddenly the arrow popped loose. The momentum shot me back and I just about fell on my butt. Thankfully, a couple of quick dance steps kept me on my feet.

"Nice moves, although it would have been more fun to see you fall," Crystal said from over by the tent.

Ignoring her and satisfied that my bow was sighted in, I decided to give shooting a rest. I went back to the tent and stood with Crystal as we looked out over the giant space. We were right in the middle of a huge, tundra-looking field with a bunch of red and green sage grass. They call it sage grass but it is nothing like grass. It is more like spongy foam than grass. Across and behind us were two huge hills that seemed to stretch out for miles. The openings between the plush pine trees glowed with fall colors: brilliant reds, oranges, yellows. There were a lot of openings, especially higher up where the trees seemed to not grow. A ways downhill from us we saw the glimmer of water through the spread out pine trees. It had to be a small creek or river and I was excited to go exploring to check it out. Each end of the valley seemed to go on for miles.

"It's right about now when a person feels really small," I said to Crystal.

"You're not kidding. We are in the middle of nowhere. This is so neat! We are really lucky that Dad takes us on adventures like this. Not many kids get to experience this stuff or see places like this," she said.

"That's for sure," I replied.

"Let's go take a walk and check this place out," I suggested.

"Isn't it getting late?" Crystal asked.

"I have no idea what time it is after all this traveling," I replied. "Hey Dad," I shouted to him. "What time is it? And what time does it get dark around here?"

"It's 8:35," he answered from inside the tent. "Mitch told me it doesn't get dark around here until 10:15 or so. And then we can see again around 6:30 in the morning."

"Wow, that's a lot of hunting time. Do you care if we go do a little exploring?" I asked.

"We can't hunt until tomorrow, but if you guys want to take a short walk around the field that would be fine. Don't get carried away, it's going to be dark soon," Dad said.

"Got it! We'll be back within the hour," I replied.

Crystal and I headed down the valley in the same direction the plane flew in. The farther we got away from the tent the smaller I felt. We were both looking back once in a while, making sure the tent was still in view. We came over a little knoll and then the field gradually sloped down. We could now see where the field ended and the brush began.

"We are not going off this field without a gun," Crystal said convincingly.

"I'm with you. I just wanted to see if we could find any fresh moose tracks or a game trail or something."

Just past the slope, we stopped for a moment to look around. I scanned the hillsides that surrounded us with my binoculars. The light was getting low so when I saw a black speck way up on the hill to our right, I had to focus hard to determine if it was a bear. I guided Crystal to the spot until she had it in her binoculars, too.

"That's a bear all right," Crystal said. "How neat is that?"

"Pretty cool. I bet it's eating the blueberries Mitch said cover the hillsides."

Suddenly, the cracking of a branch broke through the silence that surrounded us. We both ripped our binoculars from our eyes and looked in the direction of the sound that didn't just come out of nowhere.

"What was that?" Crystal said in a frightened whisper.

"Not sure," I replied as my eyes scanned the brush like a hawk, looking for any movement. My heart was hammering in my chest and the thought of what could have made that sound shocked my body to life.

Then we saw a small tree move as if something rubbed up against it. It was far enough away that it didn't cause an immediate panic. We both locked in on the tree. I couldn't believe my eyes when it slowly bent over and then disappeared. Suddenly it sprang back up, wobbling back and forth as it slowly settled into its original position.

"What did that?" Crystal asked.

"I'm not sure what's going on. Maybe it's a bear trying to eat the leaves." I was guessing.

"Let's get out of here! Last time I saw something like that was in the movie *Jurassic Park* and we both know how that went," Crystal said, very concerned.

"Yeah, that might be a good idea. Especially since we don't have anything to protect ourselves," I whispered back. Now I wondered what we were thinking, walking around in Alaska without any protection.

We hunched down and quickly and quietly scurried back up the small incline. When we reached the backside of the hill I dropped to my knees and lifted my binoculars, zeroing in on the area.

"What are you doing?" Crystal asked, confused.

"I really want to see what's out there," I replied.

Suddenly, the brush next to the tree began to fall over as if a small bulldozer were driving in our direction. My eyes grew bigger when out of the brush appeared two huge white antlers.

"It's a moose!" I said in an excited whisper.

Crystal was now on the ground next to me and we were both staring through our binoculars to get a good look at the moose. The light was fading fast but the giant antlers glowed as white as two shining angels hanging from its head. Suddenly it stopped walking and started to rub those

giant antlers up and down in the bushes.
Then, like a toy someone wound tight and
let go, his antlers ripped through the brush.
Like a thrashing machine, up, down, back
and forth he tore. We both gasped. The sound
and energy coming from the giant moose
sent a jolt of panic through my body. This
was intense and I had never seen anything
like it. As the branches flew over the moose's
head I felt Crystal's hand pull me up.

"Come on, you nut. We have to get out of
here!" Crystal said, very determined.

"You don't have to tell me twice. Let's
go!" I said as I popped to my feet.

We half-ran the whole way back to the
tent. Out of breath and still jacked up, I dove
into the tent and began to unload the story
on Dad. To my surprise, Dad was already in
his sleeping bag, fast asleep.

"What are you doing?" I shouted. "You can't be sleeping already! You won't believe what we just saw! It was giant! And I'm not sure my bow is going to kill something so big!"

Dad just lay there with his hands tucked under his head. He cracked one eye at me, considered me for a moment, then closed the eye again.

Crystal now joined me in explaining how impressive the whole thing was, and confirming my talk of how big the moose is. Dad just smiled and listened to us babble on.

"Sounds like we are going to have some fun tomorrow trying to find that big guy," Dad said quietly. "For now, how about we settle in and get some sleep."

"I can't go to sleep until I know who gets the first chance at the moose," I said.

"If I flip a coin will you promise me you'll go to sleep? Or at least let me go to sleep?" Dad asked.

"Definitely!"

Dad turned on the battery lantern and the tent filled with soft yellow light. He rummaged in his bag and pulled out a nickel. "This will have to do. I can't find a quarter. Okay, who's calling it?"

"Crystal, go for it. You can call it," I said.

"Okay. Heads I guess," she said.

Dad flipped the coin in the air and let it land on Crystal's sleeping bag. We both hunched over and focused in on the coin.

"YES! Tails!" I cheered.

"That's okay. You get first crack with your bow, but remember Dad and I will be right behind you with our guns," Crystal said with some confidence.

"Okay, now let's get some sleep," Dad pleaded.

We kicked off our boots and crawled into our sleeping bags. This was sure to be one of the longest nights of my life.

Chapter 6

When Dad's alarm started beeping I had already been laying awake for a half hour imagining sneaking up to that moose a hundred different ways. When Dad moved to turn off the alarm I knew he was up.

"Morning," I said.

"Top of the morning to you, buddy. You ready for a great day?"

"I was born ready."

Dad rolled over and started the camp stove burner to heat up some water. He lined up three white paper bowls and soon we were all propped on our sides eating some cinnamon spice oatmeal. There was no reason to head out of camp until we could see, because we didn't really know where we were going anyway. Also, that bull was within a half mile of camp last night.

I rolled out of my bag and pulled on my boots. I unzipped the tent and popped outside. The chilly air was refreshing and the dull light of morning was trying to fill the valley.

It didn't take us long to get dressed, packed, and ready to go. If needed, we each had plenty of food, water and survival gear to battle the Alaska wilderness. We discussed the game plan and it was clear that our main goal was to get a moose–who shot it was not as important. One moose would feed our family for a whole year. Since I had won first chance, Dad and Crystal were going to let me try with my bow. If we couldn't get close enough, then they would be ready for action.

We slowly headed across the tundra field to the spot where we'd seen the bull the night before. Crystal and I kept nodding our heads in confidence. Sure that we would see the giant moose. We made it to the top of the ridge and looked down into the brush where we had previously spotted him. We all scanned with our binoculars, searching for any sign. I glassed the hillsides around us and counted five different bears way up high. I pointed them out to Crystal and Dad and we watched them for a while.

Dad tried a few calls, doing his best to sound like a female moose. It's a funny call. You pinch your nose closed with your thumbs and start moaning long and slow like you have a bellyache. There was no action, so we started to walk into the bush hoping to see the tree that the moose beat up. After two steps off the field, we were standing in the brushy trees that now were five feet over our heads. Crystal and I looked at each other in total disbelief. Yesterday we had seen the moose's antlers over the tops. Our eyes widened at just how big that moose really was. We slithered in and found a good-sized game trail to walk. It didn't take us long to find the poor tree the moose took its aggression out on. There were broken branches as big around as my wrist and most of the bark on the trunk was peeled off. It was very cool to see.

"We should get back up on the field where we have a better view. It's way too thick in here to hunt," Dad said. Knowing he was right, we followed him through the trees and back up to the opening.

"That moose has to be around here somewhere, so let's slowly work around the field and see if we can find him," Dad said.

I have been on many hunts, and the name of the game is to stay focused and positive because exciting things can happen at any moment.

With Dad in the lead, we eased along for about an hour, like lions on the prowl. At this point we had circled halfway around the field, and our tent was still in view way off to the east. We stopped, pulled out our water bottles, and took a short break. From this location we could see another small field tucked far below us. I kept glassing it because it seemed like such a natural spot for animals to cross or graze in. On my third pass across the field, like they appeared from nowhere, two cow moose, the females, came walking out.

"Moose! Two cows just stepped out in that field down there," I said, fired up.

Both Crystal and Dad immediately lifted their binos to check them out. "Nice! Now where is that bull? He can't be far away," Dad said.

We watched the two cows walk in single file into the middle of the field. Suddenly, Crystal whisper-screamed, "There he is!"

The giant bull emerged from the pine trees. He looked like he was twice the size of the cows. "Holy molly. I see him, and he's giant," Dad said. "Game on, kids! We need to get down there while they are still in the field. Let's get moving."

As always, we trusted Dad with the lead and fell in behind him. They were about three football fields away and we had to close that distance. In a speed walk, we weaved over rotted logs and plowed through thick brush. After about one hundred yards we came upon a nice-sized game trail that seemed to head right to the field. Dad turned and gave us thumbs up. Now we could cover ground and stay silent doing it.

After about fifteen minutes it looked like the field was opening up in front of us. We were definitely getting close. Suddenly Dad slammed on the brakes and stood still. Crystal and I did the same, sensing something was up. I noticed Dad's left hand was wide open by his leg, telling us not to move. Suddenly, I heard crashing. I looked over Dad's shoulder and could see two brown butts running down the trail away from us.

Dad turned and with disappointment on his face said, "That was the two cows. They were coming right up this trail. Be ready, let's keep moving."

Gripping my bow tight, I stayed close to Dad with Crystal right behind me. The trail opened up and we could see the field below us. Then we started to hear a soft grunting sound. At first I had no idea what it was. Dad smiled at me with a thumbs up and whispered it was the bull grunting. We eased closer to the field and Dad waved me ahead of him. I tiptoed forward and then could see the giant bull standing right in the middle of the little field. I pulled out my rangefinder and ranged him. Eighty yards. Too far for my bow. I was comfortable taking a forty-yard shot at most.

I looked back at Dad and whispered, "Eighty yards."

"I will try calling him closer," Dad whispered back.

Dad started to moan like a cow moose and the bull grunted louder and started slowly rocking his head back and forth. It actually seemed like it was working. Little did we know, the two cows were standing in the woods just forty yards away watching us. They quickly realized that we were not moose and ran out into the field right past the bull without stopping. He was not about to let them get away and quickly turned and followed right behind them. Crystal ran up to the tree next to me and raised her gun. Dad kept calling desperately, hoping the bull would decide to stop or come back. Before we knew it the bull and cows were into the trees and gone.

"I didn't have an ethical shot," Crystal said in despair.

"You made the right decision. No sense taking a bad shot," Dad consoled her.

For a moment we all just sat there looking at one another. "I can't believe that just happened," I said. "Sorry guys, you could have easily taken him with your guns."

"That's hunting. You never know how it's going to shake out. Without those cows, I think we had him," Dad said.

Heartbroken but excited that we had seen moose and had a chance, we hunted for another couple of hours before we headed back to camp for lunch. After lunch and a nap, it was time to go back out with high hopes of seeing that moose again, or finding another one. We tried the same route, hoping the big guy was still in the area. We glassed the hillsides and snuck around in the bush for several hours. We ended the evening watching the small field where we had seen the moose earlier that morning. As the first day's light faded, we made our way back up the hill to camp and settled in for the night.

Chapter 7

Day two's adventure began as we headed south to explore new territory. Just as we reached the end of the field, the sun peeked over the top of the eastern slope and shined a spotlight on the western side. The red glow filled the hillside and lit up the blueberry plants. We could now see four different black bear scattered about.

"Take a look at the one on the bottom over there," Dad said.

I looked in the direction his binoculars were pointing and scanned for the bear with my binos. It didn't take me long to find him.

"That's a big bear," I said. "His head looks small for his body even from this far away."

"It's fascinating that they have no idea that we are watching them," Crystal said, now locked in on it as well.

"That bear is not that far from us. Should we head in that direction and see if we can get close to him?" Dad asked.

"What do we have to lose?" I said. "We might even stumble into a moose on our way."

We changed direction and headed into the pine trees, making our way toward the bear. He was about a half mile away so I figured it would take us roughly twenty minutes or so to get close to him. As we weaved through the trees we found a nice game trail that was easy to follow. Dad stopped after about ten minutes and looked down. "We might be getting close, and that's the darnedest thing I have ever seen."

Crystal and I crowded around Dad to see what he was looking at. It was a huge pile of bear poop that was as blue as the bluest blueberries I had ever seen.

"Besides being a little gross, that is really interesting!" Crystal said.

"Looks like Papa Smurf did his business on the trail," I joked.

Crystal and I broke out laughing and Dad quickly shushed us. We covered our mouths and laughed into our gloves. We continued up the trail and walked past three other very fresh piles. The bear were definitely using this trail. After a while the trees began to thin out and we started seeing loads of blueberries. Dad picked a few and popped them into his mouth. He gave us thumbs up so Crystal and I picked a few for ourselves. With some hesitation, Crystal put two in her mouth. Her eyes lit up and I knew that was a good sign. I tossed a few into my mouth and they tasted fantastic! Easily the biggest and sweetest blueberries I had ever eaten.

We refocused back to hunting, and began stalking slowly down the trail. Suddenly, Dad put his hand up and dropped to his knees. Crystal and I reacted immediately and crouched down as if we were hiding from the enemy. Dad slowly raised his binoculars to his eyes and gave something a good long stare. Then he lowered them and slowly crawled back to us.

"The bear is right in front of us in the next opening. He has no idea we are here," Dad said quietly. "Luke, you get in front. Let's see if you can get within bow range. He's a good bear."

Instantly my heart started to race, knowing it was go time. I gave Dad a thumbs up, then stayed low and moved forward. I needed to see the bear and figure out where he was and how I was going to get closer to him. My eyes came alive when I peeked around the corner and saw the bear's sheer black mass, about eighty yards in front of us. It looked like the trail we were on would bring me right to the bear and there were enough brush and trees to cover me.

The stalk was on. In a low crouch, I eased my way to the next clump of bushes. When I couldn't see the bear, I knew he couldn't see me, so I moved a little faster. I figured I must be within forty yards now, so I got down on my knees and started a slow army crawl. It was a little awkward with my bow in my left hand, but hunting mule deer in Alberta trained me well for this. My heart was racing and my hands were shaking each time I lifted them off the ground. I stopped for a minute to take some slow, deep breaths to calm down. I looked back and realized Dad was just a couple feet behind me. He gave me a reassuring nod and that helped me calm down some more. It was good to know Dad had my back with his rifle. I slid an arrow from my quiver and nocked it in place.

With renewed confidence I eased forward a few more yards until I felt like I was in the zone. I slowly rose to my knees, like I was re-entering the world from the underground. When I saw the pitch-black fur move in front of me it all became so real. The giant bear still had no idea we were there. The light breeze blowing right in my face and my ninja stalking skills kept me unnoticed. I carefully raised my rangefinder to my right eye and pushed the button. The red numbers inside read twenty-six yards. I was amazed that I had gotten so close. I knew that all my practice shooting would make this shot a slam dunk, even with my hands trembling. I went into shoot mode and started to talk my way through.

"Okay, you got this. Stay calm, raise up, pick your spot right behind the shoulder, hold steady, and let her fly."

I was ready. I took one last deep breath and slowly let it seep out of my nostrils. I then peeked through the brush as if I was a lion ready to pounce and made sure the bear was still in a good position. Like a perfectly tuned machine, I rose slowly and drew my arm back at the same time. I was above the brush and now, totally exposed, with my bow at full draw. The bear caught my movement and turned his head in my direction. The sight of his small head compared to his giant body confirmed again he was a shooter.

For a moment, time stood still as I locked my top pin on a spot right behind his shoulder. I squeezed my release and the arrow shot through the air like the speed of sound. The bright green fletching at the end of my arrow appeared for a split second against the solid black fur and then disappeared like a flash of light. The bear flinched and bit its side as if he was just stung by a hornet. Like a stampede of horses he bolted into the brush and crashed away.

I quickly turned to see if Dad had witnessed what just happened. He was standing with his arms raised high like he was signaling a touchdown. I raised mine up with my bow reaching for the sky. I ran over and gave him a huge high five and then dropped to my knees. My legs had suddenly turned to rubber. I put my shaking hands up to my face and grunted YES into my gloves as every muscle in my body flexed. I took a few deep breaths then Dad helped me to my feet.

"Now that was cool!" Dad said breaking the silence.

"It was clearly one of the most exciting things that has ever happened to me. The shot looked perfect, so I can't imagine he went too far," I said.

"I agree. But he did run right into that really thick stuff so that will be interesting," Dad replied.

A branch cracked and our heads whipped around quickly. We were still in high alert mode. To our relief, it was Crystal hurrying down the trail.

"Well, did you get him?" Crystal asked, a little out of breath.

"We don't have him yet, but I made a perfect shot."

"All I could see was the bear looked your way and then turned and bolted," Crystal said.

"It was unbelievable, Crystal. I snuck within twenty six yards of him. He looked giant and I can't wait to put my hands on him."

"Let's sit right here and have a snack. We'll give the bear some time and then we will go look for your arrow and blood," Dad instructed.

Chapter 8

After a wait that seemed to take forever, we put our packs back on and walked to where the bear had been standing. We quickly found a couple drops of bright red blood and I gave Dad a confident thumbs up. It's always good to see the blood since that's the only sure way of tracking an animal you have shot. Like a bloodhound, I was on the trail. It was a direct route to the edge of the thick brush where the bear had been swallowed by the vegetation.

"I think you better take the lead," I whispered to Dad. "Unless you want to give me your gun?"

"I'll go. You guys stay close, let's not lose anyone," Dad said.

Quickly the trail became jungle-thick. We were on our hands and knees, weaving through the brush. I looked back a couple of times to make sure Crystal was still behind me. She couldn't get any closer without hitting the bottom of my boots. Her face looked like it had the time we rode to the top of the biggest rollercoaster we'd ever seen. Suddenly Dad stopped, scrambled to his knees, and raised his gun. I bumped into his left boot with the end of my bow. He held motionless, so Crystal and I stayed that way, too. I cringed waiting for the gun to ring out, knowing it would be viciously loud with all the brush to hold in the sound. I could feel Crystal squeezing my left boot. Then Dad let out a long breath. "Whew. That was interesting," he said, obviously relieved.

I arched up and looked over his shoulder and could see a black blob right in front of Dad. He poked at it with his gun barrel and then looked back at Crystal and me.

"It's a good thing he's dead, because I'm not sure where we would have run to if he moved," Dad said letting out a relieved breath of air. "Well, you got him. Now we have to figure out how to get this beast out in the open!"

I pushed my way past Dad and carefully crawled up to the giant bear. I patted it on the butt, excited to get my hands on him and to make sure he was really dead before I got too close to him. His musty, barnyard smell hung in the air around us.

Dad unloaded his gun and slid it back to Crystal. She crawled up and grabbed my bow as well. "I'll carry these. You guys get the fun of dragging that bear."

None of us were excited about being jammed in the underbrush like this. So not wanting to waste any time, Dad and I grabbed the bear's back legs and began heaving him out. It was awkward and took everything we had to drag him a couple of feet with each tug. Crystal stayed right in front of us the whole way out. By the time we made the final pull and the bear was clear of the brush, Dad and I collapsed on our backs, dripping with sweat and gasping for air.

After catching my breath, I popped up to take a good look at my trophy. He was a true beauty. My hands sunk deep in his thick black coat which was ready for the cold Alaska winter. His paws dwarfed my hands and his claws were longer than my fingers. Dad figured he weighed about four hundred pounds.

We spent the rest of the afternoon working on the bear. Dad and I skinned him so we could get a rug made to hang on the wall or lay on the floor. It took us an hour or so to remove all the meat. We divided it up into three game bags to protect it from flies, which found us almost immediately. The hard work wasn't over, as it took two trips to haul everything back to camp and to get the meat in a cooler. When we were finally done, Dad gathered up enough energy to make us some sandwiches. We ate and then we collapsed in the tent and took a well-deserved nap.

Chapter 9

We were all moving a little slow after we woke up. The evening hunt consisted of a lot of glassing and not much hiking. Other than a few black bears way up on the hills, we didn't see anything moving. We made the short walk back to camp, where Dad heated up some beef stew from a can for dinner. It was surprisingly good–it really hit the spot. We all crashed early. Obviously we needed to recharge from the long day.

As Dad's alarm went off on day number three, there was definitely a chill in the air that we had not previously felt. I reached over and grabbed my pants. With a lot of wiggling, I managed to pull them on inside my warm sleeping bag. I rolled over and pulled on my hoodie and my jacket. After some hot oatmeal Crystal unzipped the tent and the cold air poured in like a bucket of ice water. It sent a shiver over my body. I climbed out of the tent behind Crystal and was excited when I could see across the field. It was time to go hunting, and who knew what Alaska was going to serve up today!

After that first brush with the cold, we put on an extra layer to fight off the weather and then headed out. We'd gotten a bear; now we were anxious to find a moose. We marched our way across the tundra field heading west. When we reached a high point, we glassed the hillside, searching for the magical white antlers of a giant bull moose. We came up empty handed, so we journeyed on toward a small river that snaked along the bottom of the valley.

"I think we should cross over to the other side and check it out," Dad said. "What do you guys think? No reason not to."

"Nope. Sounds good, Dad," Crystal replied.

The wide-open feeling of the tundra began to collapse as we dropped lower. Before we knew it, we were standing at the edge of another jungle-like thicket. The plush river bottom was filled with twisted, tangled vine-like bushes that were well over our heads. The cold morning air seemed to be stuck here and it was noticeably damp and darker. We quickly realized that we were going to end up on our hands and knees again, just like when we were searching for my bear. Dad was leading, Crystal was in the middle, and I was in back. As we weaved our way through the maze the sound of the river grew louder. Suddenly the cracking of a branch caused us all to freeze. With the sound of the bubbling water our senses were off and it was hard to figure out what direction the crack came from. Dad looked back at Crystal and pointed to his ear, asking if she had heard what he heard. She nodded her head. He pointed to our left to see if she agreed on the direction of the sound. She shrugged her shoulders and shook her head. It was clear none of us knew what direction the sound came from. With eyes full of fear, Crystal looked back at me and I shook my head too. We all knew we were in no position to defend ourselves from whatever it was.

With a whole new urgency, Dad began to scurry forward. We came to the river and rose quickly, looking both ways. Dad crunched his shoulders, indicating he had no idea what had made the noise. We busted our way through the last few yards of brush, forgetting about being quiet. When we made it to the other side it was like entering another world. The light returned, the tundra grass was quiet and a calm came back over me. We followed Dad up the hill and the higher we climbed, the more we could see. After we were halfway up, we stopped to do some glassing. I could see our tent in plain view, sitting motionless in the field way across from us.

I was taking a break from my binoculars when something caught my eye. I looked down by the river and saw a black bear standing there looking around.

"Check it out! There's a bear down there," I pointed.

Crystal and Dad both turned to see the bear. Then it started to walk out in the open and out popped two small cubs. "How cute is that!" Crystal said.

"Pretty cute, Crystal, from here, that is. I have a feeling that's what made the noise down by the river," Dad said. "I think we are very lucky she decided to run and not defend her cubs."

"Oh! You're right. That could have been bad," she replied.

"Guys, don't move! There's a cow moose," I whispered.

About a football field away a big cow moose had appeared and was walking in our direction. Dad and Crystal slowly turned their heads, dying to see it. We were stuck in the middle of nothing and had nowhere to hide.

"Stay low and let's hope a bull is right behind her," Dad said.

We all eased down on to our left sides. Propped up by my left elbow I could keep my binoculars up and watch this beautiful animal. Looking lanky and tall with dark caramel color fur, she was in no hurry as she walked and ate. We waited patiently and kept a close eye in all directions, waiting and hoping for a bull moose to show himself. Before we knew it, the cow was walking right to us.

"Oh my, get down guys. We don't want to spook her," Dad whispered.

Not believing what was happening, we all rolled over. I crossed my hands under my chin and laid flat with my eyes up. I had to see this. The cow was at a slight decline from us so I could only see the top of her head. A few minutes later I could see her full head and chest as she moved closer.

Still not believing this was happening, I watched her walk up the slope and stand just ten steps away from us. She had no idea the three clumps in the tundra grass were breathing. She was so close I could hear her chewing and see the shine in her eyes.

This was a moment I will never forget! Then I wondered how many people ever get to experience anything like this?

We lied there and watched her eat and mosey around for over an hour. I had to lay my head down several times to give my neck a break. Thank goodness the tundra was soft. She finally slipped back into the trees and disappeared.

"How awesome was that!" Crystal said.

"Amazing!" I replied.

"We are very lucky to have witnessed that. How many people do you think get that close to a moose?" Dad asked.

"I was laying there wondering the same thing," I said with a grateful smile.

"Not many," Crystal replied. "We'll be telling this story for a long time."

We spent the whole rest of the day on the new side looking for a bull moose, not even going back for lunch. As the sun dropped below the western hill we made our way back down to the river. Not knowing where the mom and cubs had gone, we were like African wildebeest sneaking through the grass wondering if a lion was near. We didn't waste any time and were very relieved when we popped through to our side.

Chapter 10

Sometime in the middle of the night the wind and rain started to pound on the tent. The whipping tent walls and the relentless hammering of rain drops woke me up. I rolled over, covered my head and went back to sleep. Later I woke to the muffled sound of Dad and Crystal talking.

"What's going on?" I asked tiredly.

"It's wicked outside," Crystal said.

"I think we better let the storm pass before we head out," Dad said, lying on his back in his sleeping bag.

"Bummer! Well, I'm going back to sleep then. Wake me if it clears up," I said as I rolled over.

I woke up a few hours later and now could see inside the tent. It was by no means bright and the rain and wind were still thrashing on the outside. Dad and Crystal were reading their books.

"It's about time you woke up. You have been snoring for hours," Crystal said.

"What time is it?" I asked.

Dad looked at his watch. "10:00 and you missed breakfast."

"Wow! Still bad out?"

"Yep," Dad said. "Welcome to Alaska. They warned us about the weather."

I pulled out *The Lord of The Rings*, found my spot and dove in. After an hour or so I realized I was getting hungry. "What's for lunch? I'm starving."

"Well, let me dig around and see what we have," Dad said. "Hey, there's a couple cans of Spam here. How about a hot Spam sandwich?"

"What the heck is Spam?" Crystal asked.

"Oh, you guys will love it. I had it a bunch when I was a kid. It's kind of like ham mixed with something. No one knows for sure what it is, but it tastes good," Dad said convincingly.

He cut the Spam into three thick slices and tossed them onto the frying pan. They sizzled and filled the tent with the mouthwatering smell of ham and bacon together. My mouth was watering in anticipation of that first bite. Dad directed me to get the bread out and put some mayo on six slices. He slid the fried Spam onto the bread and Crystal and I had our first Spam sandwiches. They were as good as advertised.

The day dragged on and the wind and rain were relentless. We played a bunch of games of cards and even got to the point of playing I Spy, like when we were kids on a long drive. It was turning into one of the longest days ever. Twice I tried putting my raingear on and going out, but every time quickly realized it was a bad idea. The wind and rain were just too strong. Plus I had to deal with all my wet stuff back in the tent. It was a total bummer, but staying positive was the only good choice we had. One thing I have learned is when you are on an adventure, you have to take what is dealt and go with it.

It wasn't until one in the afternoon the next day when the rain finally gave up. We looked at each other, realizing peaceful silence refilled the tent. With renewed optimism, I unzipped the flap, peeked outside and could see the blue sky coming. We put on our hunting clothes and crawled out of the tent. The ground underneath my boots felt like an overfilled sponge. My body was taking its own sweet time adjusting to being upright again. Both Dad and Crystal were working through some stretches, loosening their bodies up. Dying to make up for lost time, we grabbed our gear and headed out looking for a moose.

Counting the days in my head, I began to get a little discouraged. It was already day number five of our seven days of hunting. That didn't leave much time for us to get one moose, and there were three of us with moose tags. I quickly put that out of my mind, and reminded myself that this whole adventure had already been amazing.

Circling the end of the tundra, we began hearing a strange sound and we all tilted our heads trying to let it sink in. I looked at Dad, "Is that a plane?"

"I think you're right," Dad said.

We stared up into the blue sky and searched for movement as the sound grew louder. "There it is!" Crystal shot out, sounding like she'd just won I Spy.

It was Mitch, and he was heading right to our camp. We kept an eye on the plane as we marched back up to the top of the field. He circled once and then, like a duck dropping into a pond, he landed. We had some ground to cover so we picked up the pace and hoofed it back to camp. I was excited to talk with Mitch because there was so much to tell him. The bull moose encounter, the bear I shot, the cow moose that got so close to us, the crazy storm. Then it occurred to me that he had been flying and I wondered what he has seen from the sky.

"Howdy!" Mitch said as we approached.

"Hi Mitch," Dad shot back.

"Well, who shot this dandy black bear? The hide looks nice," Mitch said.

"I got that guy with my bow! It was totally sick."

"How could you tell he was sick?" Mitch looked confused.

"Kid talk. Sick is a good thing," Dad said with a half-smile.

"Got it," Mitch smiled back.

We went on and on with Mitch as we got caught up on the last five days. We peppered him with questions on hunting techniques, were we looking in the right spots, had he seen anything from the sky. He told us the big bull was still in the area and there were a couple others, too. Since we only had two days left, he recommended we hike over to Mel and Reed's camp and team up with them. He explained that if one of us shot a moose, the five of us working together could get it back to camp in time. He also said there were some really good spots for moose to hang out between our two camps. One big meadow in particular. He said we'd know it when we saw it. It was a big bowl where you could sit up on top and glass the whole area below.

That was all that we needed to hear to get excited about a new plan. Dad and Mitch talked over the route. Dad was concerned that Mitch didn't have coordinates for us to put into our handled GPS units. He asked him several times how we were going to find the camp. Mitch kept telling him that the runway was huge over there and we couldn't miss it. He pointed to a big hill off in the distance and told us to head straight for that hill, the runway was just below it.

I could sense Dad's doubt by the way he looked out at the hill and then back at Mitch. "Mm, you really think we can find it?"

"You can't miss it," Mitch assured us.

I could see the excitement for a new adventure in Dad. Dad loves adventures and challenges, and this was both. The plan was unfolding. Mitch told us to pack some extra food and water for the hike. He explained he would drop our sleeping bags and gear off at the other camp, and let Mel and Reed know we were heading their way. Crystal, Dad, and I gathered our stuff like squirrels packing nuts for winter. In thirty minutes we were geared up and ready.

Chapter 11

Like a small team of army soldiers finding their way back to base, we headed out. Dad led us over the tundra and down the hill toward the first river crossing. In a short time we were all on our hands and knees crawling through the jungle-thick brush. We popped out the other side, climbed back on our feet and forged ahead without hesitating. Dad's quick pace confirmed to me that we weren't hunting; we were on a mission to get where we needed to go. We couldn't see the hill because we'd been swallowed up by the trees and brush. Dad kept a close eye on his compass and made sure we were heading due west.

After about an hour and a half of hiking, crawling, and several swamp crossings, Dad finally stopped and we took a much-needed break. I wiped off the sweat dripping down my forehead so it wouldn't get in my eyes. After holding my water bottle on my neck for a few seconds I took a giant gulp. I could feel it travel all the way through my body, cooling my core as it went. This was one of those times when water tasted so good. I was careful only to take a few big swigs because this water had to last me.

"According to Mitch, we should be getting close. This is getting interesting, since we can't even see the hill anymore," Dad said.

"Are you sure we can find it, Dad?" Crystal asked.

"We really don't have a choice now. We are committed to this crazy adventure," Dad replied.

"We'll make it. Don't you worry, Crystal. Dad and I will get you there," I said confidently.

We slid our water back in our packs and pushed along, weaving through the openings until we started to climb up a long, gradual hill. It seemed like we were approaching the top when I could see the horizon stretching out and seemingly dropping off the other side. As we got closer Dad eased up and with each slow step seemed to get smaller, like he was sneaking up on whatever was on the other side. He peeked over as he dropped to his knees. Crystal and I followed his lead. I felt like I was looking into a whole new world.

"I know if I were a moose, this is where I would be," Dad said.

"This is amazing. It must be the place Mitch was talking about," Crystal said.

We looked out over a huge valley. It had plush green grass covering every inch and a big pond at the bottom. It was very different from the red tundra grass we had been walking on and hunting over by our camp. There was no question a moose and just about any other animal would love this area.

"We have to spread out and sit here for a while. We can't be far from the camp," Dad said.

Dad didn't have to work very hard at convincing me. Crystal, on the other hand, thought it would be a good idea to find the camp first and then come back. Dad and I worked our persistent magic and finally convinced Crystal to buy into the plan.

Crystal stayed put as Dad and I moved in opposite directions from her. I found a big game trail that came from the pine trees and dropped over the edge into the valley. It seemed like a perfect spot for me to set up with my bow. I sat down with a big pine at my back. I could see into the woods and down into the valley, which made my position ideal.

I sat on high alert for about an hour. Then I caught movement below me and quickly pulled up my binoculars. I saw a black timberwolf sneaking through the brush. He popped out on a game trail below me and stood there for a couple seconds. It was very cool to see. Then he slid back into the brush and was gone.

Every once in a while I could hear Dad's moaning moose call. Eventually I noticed the light was fading and I peeked around the tree. To my surprise the sun had dropped below the hills to the west. An uneasy feeling crept over my body as I realized we really had no idea where Mel and Reed's camp was. I decided to give up my post and sneak back to Crystal.

"Hey Crystal, how's it going?" I whispered.

"Fine. I can't believe we didn't spot something down there," she said.

"No kidding. It seems perfect here. Did you see the wolf?"

"No. Shoot! That would have been exciting to see," Crystal said.

"Don't you think we better get Dad moving and find their camp?" I asked.

"Absolutely."

I waved at Dad to get his attention. He must have been watching us or sensed our concern, because he instantly started moving our way. "Are you guys getting nervous yet?" Dad asked as he walked up.

"Yeah, I think sleeping with the bears would be a bad idea," Crystal said.

"It wouldn't be a bad thing to find the camp while we can still see," I added.

"Okay, okay, we'll get moving. This place is almost too good to leave."

Dad checked his compass and locked in on west. We walked the top of the ridge, still keeping a close eye on the valley below for moose. After a short time we were back in the thick stuff again and walking was a struggle. We weaved, ducked, and pushed our way through thickets. It wasn't long and Dad stopped. "We better get our headlamps out. It seems like this might get more interesting in the dark." Crystal and I pulled our packs off and quickly found our lights. I turned my hat around and slid my headlight on. The beam bounced brightly off of two big white birch trees nearby. We have birch trees at home, but these were the first I had seen in Alaska. I peeled off some of the paper-like bark and put it in my backpack.

"What are you doing?" Crystal asked.

"This stuff works great for building fires. You never know, we might need it later," I said.

"That's not a bad idea Luke. Good thinking," Dad said.

We loaded back up and continued to follow Dad, who wasn't showing any sign of worry. Our journey went on and on until our headlights were cutting through the dark. I thought it was kind of cool as I noticed a fog of steam puffing from my mouth with each breath. Then I realized, the temperature was dropping fast. All the trees and grass around us were dripping with dew, just like we were in a rain forest. My body was steaming with sweat and I began to get a little nervous. It was going to be a long, cold night if we got stuck out here. Then I notices the sound of running water was getting louder with each step. We had to be approaching a river.

"Dad! Did Mitch say anything about crossing a river?" I asked.

"No. He definitely would have told us that," Dad said.

"You mean we are really lost?" Crystal said, the worry clear in her voice.

"Well, I know we're in Alaska. That's a good thing, right?" Dad said, trying to keep us calm with humor.

"Funny!" Crystal shot back, not amused.

"I think we should cut back and head northeast. There is a chance we went past the camp," Dad said.

Crystal and I had no idea at this point which direction to go. We had been following Dad in the pitch dark and lost all bearings and direction. "Whatever you think Dad. I am totally turned around and couldn't begin to guess what direction to go," I said.

"Let's give it a try. This is getting very interesting, and it's about right now when I question this whole program. We have no choice but to stay positive and calm. One way or another we will either find their camp or find a spot to build a fire for the night," Dad said. "Ease up on your water drinking, we may need to make it last. Also, let's not worry about being too quiet. We don't want to surprise any bear that might be around."

"We can do this, guys. Something tells me this is going to be a good story to tell later," Crystal said.

We turned back and pushed forward, staying close enough that our lights formed a bond around us. The crazy adventure had us on our hands and knees more than we were walking, which meant we were not covering much ground. Dad kept saying "Hey bear! Here we come bear! Don't be afraid, just get out of our way!"

Dad finally stopped, after we had been hiking and crawling forever, it seemed. He checked his watch. "Well, this isn't so good.

It's already 11:00. I can't imagine what Mel and Reed are thinking right now. Guys, I am sorry, but I don't even know what direction to try anymore." It was Dad's first sign of doubt. Crystal and I sat speechless. Dad has always figured it out, and "it" was everything. At that moment Crystal's eyes lit up.

"Wait a minute! What if we shoot three shots like they taught us in gun safety class?" Crystal said.

Dad turned and looked at Crystal as if the words were hard to understand or were slowly sinking in. Then, like the light bulb went on, he said, "That's a great idea! Why didn't I think of that sooner? Okay, here's the plan. I will shoot three shots into a tree, five seconds apart, and then we have to be ready for them to shoot back and pinpoint the location." I could hear Dad's renewed confidence. He shined his headlight around until he found a large, dead tree on the ground. "Okay, fire in the hole," he shouted.

Crystal and I knew those words well. It's what we say at the practice range before every shot to give anyone around a chance to plug their ears if they didn't have ear plugs in. In perfect unison, we each covered our ears. The boom rang out and I could feel the compression in my chest. I quickly pulled my hands down as Dad ejected his shell and rechambered another. Just as he was pulling his gun up to shoot again, a shot rang out in the distance. I was caught off guard, like it was the first boom of thunder in an oncoming storm. We all looked at each other. Without saying a word, as if to freeze the sound in the air, Crystal and I both pointed in the direction of the sound. Then another shot rang out from the exact direction we were pointing.

"You're right. You have the spot nailed," Dad said. "They were obviously waiting for us to do that."

"Unbelievable! We were heading in the totally wrong direction," I said.

"Great thinking, Crystal! You just saved us a very miserable and long night," Dad said.

With new energy and determination, like a gun dog going after a down bird, we charged through the brush in the new direction. After a short period of time the brush opened up and the walking became easy again. We trekked forward with our headlights bouncing with each step.

"I can see a fire!" Dad said, like music to my ears.

Crystal and I scurried around Dad to take a look. Off in the distance flickered an unmistakable orange glow. A great sense of relief and calm poured through me. I knew we were going to be safe and the long journey was just about over for tonight. Then my relief turned to excitement as I realized I was going to see Reed and get to hear about his week of hunting. We picked up the pace and closed in on the fire.

"Howdy boys," Dad said, like we were cattle hands on a drive and found some strangers at a fire.

Mel was shaking his head in disbelief, like we were a lost dog that had finally come home.

"Well, I'm only guessing this was not your plan. Is there a story behind this late arrival?" Mel said still holding his rifle over his shoulder.

"The next time a hunting outfitter tells me to walk to another camp and says you can't miss it, remind me to decline the challenge," Dad said with a worn-out half-smile.

We stood by the blazing fire for a while recounting the details of our journey. Before our dew- and sweat-soaked clothes had a chance to fully dry, exhaustion hit like a hammer. "I have to get some dry clothes on and go to bed. I am done!" I said.

Mel kicked the logs on the fire to spread them out and doused them with the bucket of water he had sitting off to the side. The fire hissed like a snake as the flames were smothered and a billow of steam poured to the sky. Reed led the way to the waiting tent that was tucked just off the tundra in a patch of trees. Unlike our tent, theirs was protected nicely from the wind. We let Crystal go in first to get dry clothes on as the rest of us waited outside, still going over the stories from the week.

Before long we were all set and piled in to the tent, like rows of caterpillars snuggled in cocoons. I took in a long, deep breath and slowly let it out, as I sunk deep into my bag from exhaustion.

Chapter 12

The click of a lighter and the unmistakable whoompf of propane igniting woke me from a dead sleep. I raised my head up to see Mel, half out of his sleeping bag, putting a pot of water on the stove. The air that hit my face was much colder than anything I remembered from the week.

"Morning, Mel," I muttered.

"Good morning, Luke. How'd you sleep?" Mel asked.

"Like a rock."

I was already sitting up when I realized I could see everything in the tent without a flashlight.

"Is the sun up?" I asked in total confusion.

"Yep. We didn't do a very good job of getting up this morning. We must have needed the sleep," Mel said.

I could not believe that we slept in on the last day of our hunt. Panic set in and I quickly nudged Dad.

"You awake?" I asked.

"I can hear you, so I must be," Dad said.

"We have to get moving. It's our last day, we can't give up yet!" I urged.

I popped out of my bag and unzipped the tent. The freezing cold air snapped at my right hand as I reached for my boots, which I'd left outside overnight. I pulled them inside. To my amazement, they were frozen solid.

This turned into a very interesting problem. One that even Dad and Mel had never seen before. Our jackets and boots, which we left outside the tent because they were soaked, were impossible to put on. It was like someone poured them into a concrete mold as a joke. I picked my jacket up and it looked like an invisible person was inside it. Besides being very funny, it was a major setback. We had to thaw our gear before we could go hunting.

Reed and I quickly gathered a bunch of dead branches and had a nice big fire roaring in no time. Working at gathering wood helped keep us warm in the frigid air before we could warm ourselves at the fire. We carefully circled our frozen boots around the flames. We had to gauge the perfect distance, where they would thaw quickly but not burn or melt. I slowly rotated my jacket like a giant chicken on a rotisserie. It took about an hour to get our boots and jackets to the point where they were usable. Still wet, but usable.

In the meantime, Dad and Mel were whipping up a big batch of scrambled eggs and sausage. The sweet smell of maple sausage filled the air and woke my starving stomach. Mel handed me a steaming plate of food and I found myself shoveling it in as if I hadn't eaten in a week.

"That was really good! Thanks," I said sitting there with an empty but quite worn-out paper plate.

"That might have been a new world record," Mel said.

I just sat there with a big smile on my face and a happy, satisfied belly.

After this crazy start to the day, we were finally ready to go out and hunt. I was a little discouraged, because Mel and Reed had only seen two small bulls the entire week. Trying to stay positive, I reminded myself of Grandma's moto: Each day is a new day and you never know what it will bring.

It was just after noon when we finally made our way across the tundra that surrounded their tent. The area was all new to Dad, Crystal, and me, but the look and feel was very familiar. Mel led the way and the rest of us fell in behind. I sensed from the slow, deliberate pace that the group was worn out after six days of being in the Alaskan wilderness. We covered some ground, but ended up spending most of the afternoon scanning the hillsides with our binoculars. Reed was quick to point out the two spots where they had seen the small bulls. We had some excitement when Crystal spotted five caribou walking over the top of one of the hills. We had not seen caribou and the two bulls in the group were huge.

"Sure wish we had a tag for one of those, don't you Reed?" I said, binoculars stuck to my eyes, keeping a close watch on them.

"That's for sure! We could cut them off at the end of the valley and they would walk right to us," Reed said.

Reed and I plotted the whole thing out through our binoculars. The caribou eventually dropped out of our sight and our focus returned to finding a bull moose.

Our final full day of hunting ended with little excitement. We saw plenty of black bear eating blueberries on the hillsides, and the caribou were cool, but we did not see the moose we were after.

Back at camp, Reed and I revived the fire. We sat around the flames telling story after story of the week's adventures. The highlight was definitely my black bear stalk, and Reed probed for every last detail. We didn't want to believe the adventure had come to an end, but Reed, Crystal and I finally, slowly kicked dirt onto the fire. Even that process we dragged out until Dad finally pleaded with us from inside the tent to get to bed. Headlamps on, we made our way to the tent and crawled inside one at a time.

"Mitch will be here around 8:00 in the morning to get the first load," Dad said. "It will take him most of the afternoon to get all of us out of here one at a time."

"Wait a minute!" A thought hit me. "Does that mean that we could actually go out hunting in the morning?"

"I was wondering when one of you kids would realize that," Mel said, tucked deep in his sleeping bag.

"Technically, there is time. Realistically, we would be in a major bind if we killed a moose on the last day and had to get it out," Dad explained.

"I like the technically part of that comment," Reed piped in. "Luke, we totally are getting up in the morning!"

"Crystal, are you in?" I asked.

"Absolutely," she said.

"All right, all right. Get some sleep. You kids can get up, but you need to stay in the field and can only shoot one if it's close to camp," Dad said.

"Sweet!" I slid into my sleeping bag with new excitement. It was as if I heard school was cancelled because of a snowstorm. Being dead tired, even with the renewed hope, I crashed to sleep in minutes.

Chapter 13

When Crystal's travel alarm clock rang out, BEEP, BEEP, BEEP, we didn't actually jump out of bed, but we did manage to get up. I turned on one of the lanterns and it filled the tent with warm, yellow light. As if we had been in battle for several days, it took extra effort to get our worn-out bodies dressed. I grabbed us the last three cinnamon bagels out of the bag. We didn't even bother putting cream cheese on them. No one had the energy.

Holding the bagel in my mouth, I crawled outside. It was different from the morning before: the chill did not hit very hard. It was the perfect morning temperature and sunlight was filling the valley.

"Come on guys, you won't believe how nice it is out here," I said.

Reed and Crystal piled out of the tent. We pulled on our backpacks and I picked up my trusty bow. Crystal and Reed each slid three shells into their guns.

"It's the fourth quarter and we are down by one touchdown. There are two minutes left and we are on the fifty-yard line. We can do this, guys" I said trying to ignite some energy.

Crystal turned in and stuck her fist out. "To luck, boys!" Reed and I both gave her a jab at the same time.

"Good call, Crystal, we could definitely use some luck right about now," Reed said with his typical big smile.

I led our new hunting group across the tundra field. It was a proud feeling knowing we were kind of on our own, even though the dads weren't that far away. After a short, brisk walk I stopped at one of the first good vantage spots.

"Crystal, do you want to post from here? Reed and I will spread out across the field so we can all see different spots," I said.

"Sure. What do I do if I see a moose?" Crystal asked.

"At this point, let's worry about that if it happens," I replied.

Crystal and Reed both accepted the answer. I am sure it was because we had only seen three bull moose in the last six days.

Reed and I continued across the spongy ground and found another spot for Reed to glass from. I moved a little farther down to where I felt like I was looking at a whole new hillside. It was that magic morning time where the light was building. Looking through my binoculars I could just start to make out the dark spots across the hills. I glassed each one slowly and carefully examining it, hoping the spot would move and prove to be an animal, not just a rock, dead log, or a bush. I scanned intensely, knowing we only had an hour or so to find a moose. This adventure of a lifetime was almost over, but I wasn't ready to give up yet.

"Gotcha." I said when I spotted my first black bear. Even though we had seen bears every day, it never got old finding that first one or two each morning. There is just something exciting about spotting an animal that has no idea you're watching it.

I heard a whistle and jerked my binoculars away from my face. I looked to my left and saw Reed and Crystal waving their arms frantically. I jumped up, grabbed my bow and ran over to them. By the looks in their eyes I could tell something exciting was happening.

"What's going on?" I said in a loud whisper. It was a question that I already knew the answer to because Crystal's face looked like she had just seen Santa come down the chimney. But it wasn't Santa we were after.

"A moose! A giant moose! I spotted a giant moose and it's close!" Crystal said as fast as I had ever heard her talk.

"Awesome! Where is he?" I asked, dying to get my eyes on him.

"Come on! Follow me!" Crystal grabbed my arm and just about dragged me along. I shot a look at Reed to make sure he was behind me. The fire in his eyes said it all. It was Go Time and we both knew it. This was what we lived for.

As we came over a slight ridge, Crystal hit the brakes and crouched down. Reed and I immediately slid in next to her. She raised her binoculars and looked down the hill. I followed the direction her binoculars were pointing and franticly scanned back and forth with my bare eyes.

"There he is! He hasn't gone very far at all!" Crystal said. "He's right on the edge of the opening in that little clearing." She pointed and I immediately pulled up my binoculars and zeroed in on the field. I slowly followed the field edge and like magic the giant moose appeared.

"Got him!" Reed said beating me to the call.

"I'm on him!" I said.

"He is giant." Reed added.

"I told you guys he was huge," Crystal shot back.

I lowered my binoculars and like a field general scanned the terrain, figuring out a game plan.

"What do you guys think about sneaking over to those trees and then moving in behind him?" I said, pointing.

"I think that should work," Reed said.

"I agree. And once we get closer, we have to make sure we keep the wind in our face," Crystal said.

"Yeah, one whiff of us and he'll be outta here," I said.

"That's for sure. You guys didn't smell good when we first got here, let alone now," Crystal said with her nose crunched up.

Reed and I both smiled and tapped knuckles. We were proud to smell like mountain men. "Come on you clowns. Let's go get a moose," Crystal said, taking off down the hill.

We made our way to the first line of trees and now the moose was out of sight. We closed the distance as quickly as we could without making too much noise. I found a worn-down game trail that seemed to head right for our field. It was easy walking and we covered the distance in no time at all. My heart rate started to pick up as the opening to the small field came into view through the trees. I instinctively crouched lower and slowed my pace. I looked back to get confirmation that Crystal and Reed approved of my path. The look on Crystal's face was priceless. It was somewhere between scared to death and total excitement. But the double thumbs up confirmed that we were all on the same page. I continued to lead our charge.

I could see the edge of the field about thirty steps in front of us, so I stopped. I lifted my binos and peered through the trees, scanning the field. I wanted to pinpoint the moose. Slowly and carefully I glassed back and forth but could not spot the unmistakable chocolate-brown fur. I looked back at Crystal and Reed and raised my shoulders and shook my head. Reed gave me a backhand wave, encouraging me to move forward. I cringed, not totally confident we should get closer without knowing where the moose was. But Crystal gave me a nod and a "why not?" look on her face.

I turned around and faced the challenge head-on. I tiptoed along the trail and eased closer to the field. Like an eagle that hadn't eaten in days, I scanned, looking for movement. I took a long deep breath and slowly let it out. My heart was racing. I knew that moose was close.

We got to the edge of the field and I felt like we were entering an elephant graveyard or something. It didn't seem like we were supposed to be this close. That moose had been standing right on the other side just twenty minutes ago. I didn't want him to smell us or hear us. I didn't know what to do. Crystal and Reed were crouched next to me and we were searching the entire field with our eyes.

"He has to be close, don't you think?" I said, so quiet they could barely hear me.

They both just nodded, not wanting to make any noise. Then, like a lightning bolt shooting through my heart, an unbelievable crashing noise filled the air. Crystal's gasp startled me almost as much. We all crunched and ducked, not knowing if a giant tree was falling on us or what was happening.

Instinctively I covered my head with my left hand as I tried to process the sound.

Crystal grabbed my arm, as if to use me as a shield.

"It's the moose!" Crystal whispered directly into my ear. At that distance it might as well have been a shout.

At that moment everything became clear. The sound continued and it was the unmistakable sound of a giant moose destroying a small tree with his massive antlers. We'd heard the same racket our first night out. Reed moved in and pointed across the field.

"The bull's right in there," he said.

"What should we do?" Crystal asked.

In the heat of the moment, I am usually pretty good at coming up with a plan. I quickly went through all the hunting shows

I had watched and all the stories I had read about moose hunting. It came to me in a flash.

"Crystal, get your gun ready. Reed, you're backing her up. She spotted him so she gets the first crack. I'm going to move back a few steps and start racking a tree with a dead branch. It works on the hunting shows, let's give it a try. All we need is for that moose to show himself." Reed and Crystal slid into ready position.

I set my bow down and picked up a big dead branch. Desperate to make something happen, I began rubbing it up and down on the bark of a pine tree. After a couple of seconds I stopped to listen for the bull. To our surprise, the thrashing sound got louder.

"You're making him mad," Reed said. "Keep it up!"

I started racking with more intensity. Then I broke some branches and really started getting into it. I was determined to convince this moose I was the real deal. As I ran out of steam I broke one more branch and then stopped. It was surprisingly quiet all of a sudden. Then we heard this grunting sound like a weightlifter picking up heavy dumbbells, one after the other. It had to be the bull moose. Then, like a gladiator stepping into the stadium, the giant appeared.

He was rocking back and forth, grunting, and slowly marching right at us. His massive antlers rocked back and forth as if he had two oak trees stuck to his head. I watched in total amazement. Crystal and Reed had their guns up and ready. Because he was facing us, Crystal did not have a good shot. We all knew he had to turn sideways so she could take a clean kill shot at his heart or lungs.

Then the moose stopped, only forty or so steps away and stared right at us. I had an amazing view. Crystal and Reed were both kneeling down five steps in front of me and the bull was standing out in the middle of the field. He was trying to locate his challenger and I got the feeling he was beginning to sense something wasn't right. He stopped grunting and was now looking back and forth as if he were scanning the trees for another moose. Then he turned broadside and looked back at us.

"Take him!" I whispered loud enough for Crystal to hear.

BOOM! Crystal's gun rang out.

The bull flinched. I am not sure if it was from the bullet or the sound. But he did not run. "Reed, shoot!" I said out loud.

Reed's gun barked and the bull flinched again. I could now see a patch of pure red blood building from the prefect spot behind his shoulder. The bull took two steps before toppling over like a giant redwood tree crashing to the ground.

Not knowing if I should break the silence, I ran to Crystal and Reed and with a hand on each of their backs I pulled them to their feet.

"You did it, you did it, you did it!" I said, trying to hold myself back from screaming. Crystal and Reed both had their mouths half open and their eyes wide as saucers.

"Say something!" I said to Crystal.

"Oh my goodness. Did that just happen?" She said looking more shocked than excited.

Moving on to Reed, I gave him a high five that just about sent him flying.

"Come on, let's go check him out." I said pushing Reed and Crystal along.

We all looked in the direction of the massive moose lying perfectly still in the grass. "Keep your guns ready, just in case.

But I don't think he's going anywhere," I said as we cautiously made our way to the moose.

The closer we got the more impressive he looked. "You go poke him," Crystal said to Reed. She clearly wanted no part in making sure he was dead. Reed slowly eased around to the right side of the giant and poked his gun barrel in his side. With a sigh of relief, Reed put his arms to the sky.

"We did it! Yes!"

Reed and Crystal set their guns off to the side and we all stared in total amazement. The moose looked so much bigger up close. It seemed like we were looking at a dump truck lying on its side. Crystal tried to pick up the giant rack and could not budge it. Reed stepped in and the two of them tried to lift it. They managed to straighten the big bull's head but could not lift it up. It was a giant. I ran my bare hands over the musty, thick hide. I couldn't believe we were actually touching a real Alaskan moose.

"Check it out guys," I said. "Two perfect shots."

Indeed, there were two small holes in the moose's hide, filled with blood. They were within three inches of each other.

Reed high-fived Crystal. "I was glad to help."

I heard a noise, and turned to see Dad and Mel weaving their way through the trees. We all three stood up.

"Victory!" Crystal raised her arms up and yelled.

"Unbelievable! Did you get him, Crystal?" Dad asked.

"Reed and I both got him. Well, actually, it was a full team effort. Luke called him in, I took the first shot and Reed followed up. It was one of the most exciting things I have ever been a part of," Crystal was beaming.

Mel grabbed the antlers. "Holy cow, this is a giant moose. You guys are awesome. Way to stick with it and not give up!"

"Well guys, let's get some pictures of this amazing animal and then we have to get moving," Dad said.

Chapter 14

After taking a bunch of pictures the work began. Mel and Dad skinned the hide so we could take it to a taxidermist and have the moose head mounted. This incredible animal deserves to be hung on a wall so we can honor it for years to come. Reed and I worked together to remove the hindquarters so we could get the meat ready for the plane. The job wasn't easy, as they weighed as much as we did. Crystal, Reed, and I teamed up to drag the quarters up to the edge of the tundra field. We hoped Mitch would be able to get the plane close enough to load the meat in. We didn't want to move it any farther than we had to.

Our final day in the Alaska wilderness ended in pure exhaustion. It took Mitch six flights to get all of us, the meat, and our gear back to base camp. Our journey home continued with two more flights and an overnight in a motel without any heat.

It didn't matter. When we arrived home in Minnesota we walked off the final plane drained like warriors back from a month long battle—but a battle that we won. As with any great adventure, the memories will last a lifetime, our bond of friendship deepened, and the stories will continue to be told.

Other books in the series

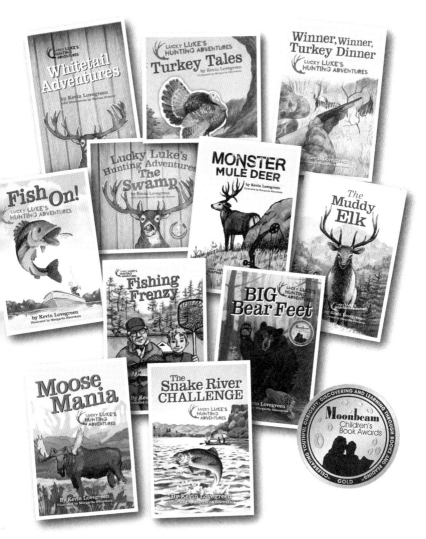

To order books, sign up for book alerts, or to see great pictures visit:

www.KevinLovegreen.com

A note to the reader,

All the stories in the Lucky Luke's Hunting Adventures series are based on real experiences that happened to me or my family.

If you like the book, please help spread the word by telling all your friends!

Thanks for reading!
Kevin Lovegreen